Born in 1999

by

Kerry Butters.

Born in 1999.

Millennium: 2nd millennium

Centuries: 19th century – **20th century** – 21st century

Decades: 1960s 1970s 1980s – **1990s** – 2000s 2010s 2020s

Years: 1996 1997 1998 – **1999** – 2000 2001 2002

1999 (MCMXCIX) was a common year starting on Friday (dominical letter C) of the Gregorian calendar, the 1999th year of the Common Era (CE) and *Anno Domini* (AD) designations, the 999th year of the 2nd millennium, the 99th year of the 20th century, and the 10th and last year of the 1990s decade.

1999 was designated as:

International Year of Older Persons.

Contents

January

- January 1 – The euro is established.
- January 4 – Gunmen open fire on Shia Muslims worshiping in a mosque in Islamabad, Pakistan, killing 16 and injuring 25.
- January 10
  - Sanjeev Nanda kills 3 policemen in New Delhi with his car, an act for which he is later acquitted, resulting in a sharp drop in public confidence in the Indian legal system.
  - *The Sopranos* debuts on HBO.
- January 20 – The China News Service announces new government restrictions on Internet use aimed especially at Internet cafés.
- January 21 – In one of the largest drug busts in American history, the United States Coast Guard intercepts a ship with over 9,500 pounds (4.75 tons) of cocaine aboard headed for Houston.
- January 25 – The 6.2 Mw Armenia, Colombia earthquake hits western Colombia, killing at least 1,000.

- January 31 – *Family Guy* debuts on Fox.

February

- February 4 – Unarmed Guinean immigrant Amadou Diallo is shot dead by New York City police officers on an unrelated stake-out, inflaming race relations in the city.
- February 7 – King Hussein of Jordan dies from cancer, and his son Abdullah II inherits the throne.
- February 11 – Pluto moves along its eccentric orbit further from the Sun than Neptune. It had been nearer than Neptune since 1979, and will become again in 2231.
- February 12 – U.S. President Bill Clinton is acquitted in impeachment proceedings in the United States Senate.
- February 16
    - In Uzbekistan, an apparent assassination attempt against President Islam Karimov takes place at government headquarters.
    - Across Europe, Kurdish rebels take over embassies and hold hostages after Turkey arrests one of their rebel leaders.
- February 21 – Sanna Sillanpää shoots 4 men, killing 3 at a shooting range in Finland.
- February 22 – Moderate Iraqi Shiite cleric Mohammad Mohammad Sadeq al-Sadr is assassinated.
- February 23
    - Kurdish rebel leader Abdullah Öcalan is charged with treason in Ankara, Turkey.

- White supremacist John William King is found guilty of kidnapping and killing African American James Byrd Jr. by dragging him behind a truck for 2 miles (3 km).
- An avalanche destroys the village of Galtür, Austria, killing 31.
- February 24 – LaGrand case: The State of Arizona executes Karl LaGrand, a German national involved in an armed robbery in 1982 that led to a death. Karl's brother Walter is executed a week later, in spite of Germany's legal action in the International Court of Justice to attempt to save him.
- February 27 – While trying to circumnavigate the world in a hot air balloon, Colin Prescot and Andy Elson set a new endurance record after being aloft for 233 hours and 55 minutes.

March

- March 1
  - One of 4 bombs detonated in Lusaka, Zambia, destroys the Angolan Embassy.
  - Rwandan Hutu rebels kill and dismember 8 foreign tourists at the Buhoma homestead, Uganda.
  - The Convention on the Prohibition of Anti-Personnel Mines comes into force.
- March 2 – The brand new Mandalay Bay hotel and casino opens in Las Vegas.
- March 3 – Walter LaGrand is executed in the gas chamber in Arizona.
- March 4 – In a military court, United States Marine Corps Captain Richard J. Ashby is acquitted of the charge of

reckless flying which resulted in the deaths of 20 skiers in the Italian Alps, when his low-flying jet hit a gondola cable.

- March 12 – Former Warsaw Pact members Hungary, Poland and the Czech Republic join NATO.
- March 15 – In Brussels, Belgium, the Santer Commission resigns over allegations of corruption.
- March 21
    - Bertrand Piccard and Brian Jones become the first to circumnavigate the Earth in a hot air balloon.
    - The 71st Academy Awards are held at the Dorothy Chandler Pavilion in Los Angeles with *Shakespeare in Love* winning Best Picture.
- March 23 – Gunmen assassinate Paraguay's Vice President Luis María Argaña.
- March 24
    - NATO launches air strikes against the Federal Republic of Yugoslavia, marking the first time NATO has attacked a sovereign country.
    - A fire in the Mont Blanc Tunnel kills 39 people, closing the tunnel for nearly 3 years.
- March 25 – Enron energy traders allegedly route 2,900 megawatts of electricity destined for California to the town of Silver Peak, Nevada, population 200.
- March 26
    - The Melissa worm attacks the Internet.
    - A Michigan jury finds Dr. Jack Kevorkian guilty of second-degree murder for administering a lethal injection to a terminally ill man.
- March 27 – Kosovo War: A U.S. F-117 Nighthawk is shot down by Serbian forces.

- March 28 – The animated sci-fi TV sitcom *Futurama* debuts on FOX.
- March 29 – For the first time, the Dow Jones Industrial Average closes above the 10,000 mark, at 10,006.78.

April

- April 1 – Nunavut, an Inuit homeland, is created from the eastern portion of the Northwest Territories to become Canada's third territory.
- April 5
    - Two Libyans suspected of bringing down Pan Am Flight 103 in 1988 are handed over to Scottish authorities for eventual trial in the Netherlands. The United Nations suspends sanctions against Libya.
    - In Laramie, Wyoming, Russell Henderson pleads guilty to kidnapping and felony murder, in order to avoid a possible death penalty conviction for the apparent hate crime killing of Matthew Shepard.
- April 7
    - Kosovo War: Kosovo's main border crossings are closed by Yugoslav forces to prevent Kosovo Albanians from leaving.
    - A bomb explodes at the Valley of the Fallen Church in Spain; GRAPO claims responsibility.
- April 8 – Bill Gates' personal fortune makes him the wealthiest individual in the world due to the increased value of Microsoft stock.
- April 9 – Ibrahim Baré Maïnassara, president of Niger, is assassinated.

- April 13 – Tercentenary celebrations of the creation of the Sikh Khalsa are held.
- April 14
  - Kosovo War: NATO warplanes repeatedly bomb ethnic Albanian refugee convoys for 2 hours over a 12-mile stretch of road, after mistaking them for Serbian military trucks, between Đakovica and Dečani in western Kosovo, killing at least 73 refugees.
- April 17 – A nail bomb, planted by David Copeland, explodes in the middle of a busy market in Brixton, South London.
- April 18 – Wayne Gretzky retires as a player from the National Hockey League.
- April 20 – Columbine High School massacre: Two Littleton, Colorado teenagers, Eric Harris and Dylan Klebold, open fire on their teachers and classmates, killing 12 students and 1 teacher, and then themselves.
- April 25 – The term of Tuanku Jaafar ibni Almarhum Tuanku Abdul Rahman as the 10th Yang di-Pertuan Agong of Malaysia ends.
- April 26
  - Sultan Salahuddin of Selangor, becomes the 11th Yang di-Pertuan Agong of Malaysia.
  - British TV presenter Jill Dando, 37, is shot dead on the doorstep of her home in Fulham, London.
- April 30
  - Cambodia joins the Association of Southeast Asian Nations (ASEAN), bringing the total members to 10.
  - A third nail bomb (see April 17) explodes in The Admiral Duncan pub in Old Compton Street, Soho,

London, killing a pregnant woman and two friends and injuring 70 others, including her husband. This is part of a hate campaign against ethnic minorities and gay people by David Copeland.

May

- May 1 – *SpongeBob SquarePants* debuts on Nickelodeon. It becomes the longest running animated children's TV show on channel to date.
- May 2 – Norman J. Sirnic and Karen Sirnic are murdered by serial killer Ángel Maturino Reséndiz in Weimar, Texas.
- May 3
  - 1999 Oklahoma tornado outbreak: A devastating tornado, rated F5 on the Fujita scale, slams into southern and eastern Oklahoma City metropolitan area, killing 36 people (+5 indirectly).
  - The Dow Jones Industrial Average closes above 11,000 for the first time, at 11,014.70.
- May 5 – Microsoft releases Windows 98 (Second Edition), from 1998.
- May 6 – Elections are held in Scotland and Wales for the new Scottish Parliament and National Assembly for Wales.
- May 7
  - A jury finds *The Jenny Jones Show* and Warner Bros. liable in the shooting death of Scott Amedure, after the show deceived Jonathan Schmitz into appearing on a secret same-sex crush episode.
  - Kosovo War: In the Federal Republic of Yugoslavia, 3 Chinese embassy workers are killed and 20 others

wounded when a NATO B-2 aircraft mistakenly bombs the Chinese Embassy in Belgrade.
- In Guinea-Bissau, President João Bernardo Vieira is ousted in a military coup.
- May 8 – Nancy Mace becomes the first female cadet to graduate from The Military College of South Carolina.
- May 12 – David Steel becomes the first Presiding Officer (Speaker) of the modern Scottish Parliament.
- May 13 – Carlo Azeglio Ciampi is elected President of Italy.
- May 17 – Ehud Barak is elected prime minister of Israel.
- May 19 – *Star Wars: Episode I – The Phantom Menace* is released in theaters. It becomes the highest grossing *Star Wars* film until *The Force Awakens* 16 years later.
- May 26
  - The Indian Air Force launches an attack on intruding Pakistan Army troops and mujahideen militants in Kashmir.
  - The first Welsh Assembly in over 600 years opens in Cardiff.
  - The 1999 UEFA Champions League Final takes place at the Camp Nou Stadium, Barcelona in which the English side Manchester United defeats the German side Bayern Munich 2-1.
- May 27 – The International Criminal Tribunal for the former Yugoslavia in The Hague, Netherlands indicts Slobodan Milošević and four others for war crimes and crimes against humanity committed in Kosovo.
- May 28
  - Swedish police officers Robert Karlström (30) and Olov Borén (42) are wounded by 3 bank robbers armed with

automatic weapons, and later executed with their own service pistols in Malexander, see Malexander murders.
- o After 22 years of restoration work, Leonardo da Vinci's *The Last Supper* is placed back on display in Milan, Italy.
- May 29
  - o Cathy O'Dowd, a South African mountaineer, becomes the first woman to summit Mount Everest from both the north and south sides.
  - o Nigeria terminates military rule, and the Fourth Nigerian Republic is established with Olusegun Obasanjo as president.
- May 30 – Travel Midland Metro enters public service.

June

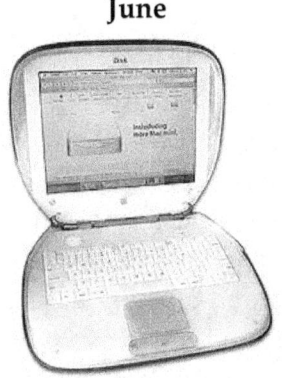

The iBook G3

- June 1
  - o Napster, a revolutionary music downloading service, debuts.
  - o American Airlines Flight 1420 overruns the runway in Little Rock, Arkansas; 11 people are killed.

- June 2 – After decades of fighting off outside technological influences like television, the King of Bhutan allows television transmissions to commence in the Kingdom for the first time, coinciding with the King's Silver Jubilee (see Bhutan Broadcasting Service).
- June 5 – The Islamic Salvation Army, the armed wing of the Islamic Salvation Front, agrees in principle to disband in Algeria.
- June 6 – In Brazil, 345 prisoners escape from Putim prison through the front gate.
- June 8 – The government of Colombia announces it will include the estimated value of the country's illegal drug crops, exceeding half a billion US dollars, in its gross national product.
- June 9 – Kosovo War: The Federal Republic of Yugoslavia and NATO sign a peace treaty.
- June 10
  - Kosovo War: NATO suspends its air strikes after Slobodan Milošević agrees to withdraw Yugoslav forces from Kosovo
  - An underground pipeline leaks 237,000 gallons (897,000 liters) of gasoline before exploding at Whatcom Falls Park in Bellingham, Washington, killing 1 adult and 2 children.
- June 12
  - Kosovo War: Operation Joint Guardian/*Operation Agricola* begins: NATO-led United Nations peacekeeping forces KFOR enter the province of Kosovo in the Federal Republic of Yugoslavia.

- o Texas Governor George W. Bush announces he will seek the Republican Party nomination for President of the United States.
- June 14 – Thabo Mbeki is elected President of South Africa.
- June 18 – The J18 international anti-globalization protests are organized in dozens of cities around the world, some of which lead to riots.
- June 19 – Turin, Italy, is awarded the 2006 Winter Olympics.
- June 30 – Twenty-three people die when fire consumes the Sealand Youth Training Center in South Korea.

July

NASA's Lunar Prospector

- July 1
  - o The Scottish Parliament is officially opened by Elizabeth II on the day that legislative powers are officially transferred from the old Scottish Office in London to the new devolved Scottish Executive in Edinburgh.
  - o Europol (short for European Police Office) the European Union's criminal intelligence agency becomes fully operational.

- July 2 – Benjamin Nathaniel Smith begins a 3-day killing spree targeting racial and ethnic minorities in Illinois and Indiana.
- July 5 – U.S. Army Pfc. Barry Winchell is bludgeoned in his sleep at Fort Campbell, Kentucky by fellow soldiers; he dies the next day from his injuries.
- July 7 – In Rome, Hicham El Guerrouj runs the fastest mile ever recorded, at 3:43.13.
- July 8 – A major flash flood in Las Vegas swamps hundreds of cars, smashes mobile homes and kills 2 people.
- July 10 – American soccer player Brandi Chastain scores the game winning penalty kick against China in the FIFA Women's World Cup.
- July 11 – India recaptures Kargil, forcing the Pakistan Army to retreat. India announces victory, ending the 2-month conflict.
- July 16 – Off the coast of Martha's Vineyard, a plane crashes piloted by John F. Kennedy Jr., killing him, his wife Carolyn Bessette-Kennedy, and her sister Lauren Bessette.
- July 20
    - Mercury program: Liberty Bell 7 - piloted by Gus Grissom in 1961 - is raised from the Atlantic Ocean.
    - Falun Gong is banned in the People's Republic of China under Jiang Zemin.
- July 22 – The first version of MSN Messenger is released by Microsoft.
- July 23
    - NASA's Chandra X-ray Observatory is launched.
    - ANA Flight 61 is hijacked in Tokyo.

- Mohammed VI of Morocco becomes king upon the death of his father Hassan II.
- July 23–July 25 – The Woodstock 99 festival is held in New York.
- July 23 – 14 Kosovo Serb villagers are killed by ethnic Albanian gunmen in the village of Staro Gračko.
- July 26 – The last Checker taxi cab is retired in New York City and auctioned off for approximately $135,000.
- July 27 – Twenty-one people die in a canyoning disaster near Interlaken, Switzerland.
- July 31 – NASA intentionally crashes the Lunar Prospector spacecraft into the Moon, thus ending its mission to detect frozen water on the lunar surface.

August

1999 İzmit earthquake, Turkey

- August 7 – Hundreds of Chechen guerrillas invade the Russian republic of Dagestan, triggering a short war.
- August 8 – The first Callatis Festival, the largest music & culture festival in Romania, is held.
- August 9 – Russian President Boris Yeltsin fires his Prime Minister, Sergei Stepashin, and for the fourth time fires his entire cabinet.

- August 10
    - Buford O. Furrow, Jr. wounds 5 and kills 1 during the Los Angeles Jewish Community Center shooting.
    - The Atlantique incident occurs as an intruding Pakistan Navy plane is shot down in India. The incident sparks tensions between the 2 nations, coming just a month after the end of the Kargil War.
- August 11
    - A total solar eclipse is seen in Europe and Asia.
    - Salt Lake City tornado: A very rare F2 tornado strikes Salt Lake City, killing 1.
- August 17 – 1999 İzmit earthquake: A 7.6-magnitude earthquake strikes İzmit and levels much of northwestern Turkey, killing more than 17,000 and injuring 44,000. This is the first of a long series of unrelated but frequent earthquakes throughout the world during the years 1999 and 2000.
- August 19 – In Belgrade, tens of thousands of Serbians rally to demand the resignation of Yugoslav President Slobodan Milošević.
- August 22
    - Mandarin Airlines Flight 642 crashes in Hong Kong.
    - GPS Week Numbers reset to 0.
- August 26 - The Second Chechen War starts
- August 30 – East Timor votes for independence from Indonesia in a referendum.
- August 31 – Apple Computer releases the Power Macintosh G4.

September

- September 7
  - A magnitude 5.9 earthquake hits Athens, killing 143 and injuring more than 2,000.
  - Viacom and CBS merge.
- September 8 – The first of a series of Russian apartment bombings occurs. Subsequent bombings occur on September 13 and 16, while a bombing on September 22 fails.
- September 9 – Sega Dreamcast is released in North America as well as Sonic Adventure.
- September 12 – Under international pressure to allow an international peacekeeping force, Indonesian president BJ Habibie announces that he will do so.
- September 14 – Kiribati, Nauru and Tonga join the United Nations.
- September 21 – The 921 earthquake, also known as the Jiji earthquake (magnitude 7.6 on the Richter scale), kills about 2,400 people in Taiwan.

October

Mars Climate Orbiter during tests

- October – NASA loses one of its probes, the Mars Climate Orbiter.
- October – Cold War: The last Russian military soldiers withdraw from the Baltic states ending Soviet/Russian military presence that lasted since 1940.
- October 1 – Shanghai Pudong International Airport opens in China, taking over all international flights to Hongqiao.
- October 5 – Thirty-one people die in the Ladbroke Grove rail crash, west of London, England.
- October 12
  - Pakistani Prime Minister Nawaz Sharif attempts to dismiss Army Chief General Pervez Musharraf and install ISI director Ziauddin Butt in his place. Senior Army generals refuse to accept the dismissal. Musharraf, who is out of the country, attempts to return in a commercial airliner. Sharif orders the

Karachi airport to not allow the plane to land. The generals lead a coup d'état, ousting Sharif's administration and taking over the airport. The plane lands with only a few minutes of fuel to spare, and Musharraf takes control of the government.

- Date selected by the UN as when the world population reaches 6 billion people.

- October 13 – The United States Senate rejects ratification of the Comprehensive Test Ban Treaty (CTBT).
- October 15 – A National Geographic Society press conference reveals the fossil of *Archaeoraptor* (which is later found to be a forgery).
- October 22 – Grand Theft Auto 2 is released on PlayStation.
- October 27 – Gunmen open fire in the Armenian Parliament, killing Prime Minister Vazgen Sargsyan, Parliament Chairman Karen Demirchyan, and 6 other members.
- October 29 – a super cyclonic storm impacts Orissa, India, killing approximately 10,000 people.
- October 31
  - EgyptAir Flight 990, travelling from New York City to Cairo, crashes off the coast of Nantucket, Massachusetts, killing all 217 on board. When the pilot leaves the cockpit, the co-pilot causes the Boeing 767 to enter a steep dive, resulting in impact with the Atlantic Ocean.
  - Roman Catholic Church and Lutheran Church leaders sign the Joint Declaration on the Doctrine of Justification, ending a centuries-old doctrinal dispute over the nature of faith and salvation.

November

- November 6 – Australians defeat a referendum proposing the replacement of the Queen and the Governor General with a President to make Australia a republic.
- November 9 – TAESA Flight 725, covering the route Tijuana–Guadalajara–Uruapan–Mexico City, crashes a few minutes after takeoff from Uruapan International Airport, killing 18 people on board. This event causes the bankruptcy of the Mexican airline a few months later.
- November 12 – A 7.2-magnitude earthquake strikes Düzce and northwestern Turkey, killing 845 and injuring 4,948.
- November 18 – The Aggie Bonfire collapses in College Station, Texas, killing 12.
- November 19 – Dr. Jerome Teelucksingh of Trinidad and Tobago proposes that the United Nations create an International Men's Day, which is now commemorated every year on this same date.
- November 20 – The People's Republic of China launches the first Shenzhou spacecraft.
- November 21 – The film *The Wizard of Oz* begins its run on cable TV, which continues to this day. On cable it is telecast several times a year, like most other films, rather than being shown only once annually.
- November 23 – The National Assembly of Kuwait revokes a 1985 law that granted women's suffrage.
- November 26 – The 7.5 Mw Ambrym earthquake shakes Vanuatu and a destructive tsunami follows. Ten people were killed and forty were injured.

- November 27 – The left-wing Labour Party takes control of the New Zealand government, with leader Helen Clark becoming the second female Prime Minister in New Zealand's history.
- November 30
    - The ExxonMobil merger is completed, forming the largest corporation in the world.
    - WTO Protests – Protesters block delegates' entrance to WTO meetings in Seattle, United States.

December

The Millennium Dome opened in London.

- December – In Cambodia, the Khmer Rouge was officially dissolved.
- December 3
    - Six firemen from Worcester, Massachusetts were killed in the Worcester Cold Storage and Warehouse fire.
    - After rowing for 81 days and 2,962 nautical miles (5486 km), Tori Murden became the first woman to cross the Atlantic Ocean by rowboat alone, when she reached Guadeloupe from the Canary Islands.

- NASA lost radio contact with the Mars Polar Lander, moments before the spacecraft entered the Martian atmosphere.
- December 18 – NASA launched the Terra platform into orbit, carrying 5 Earth Observation instruments, including ASTER, CERES, MISR, MODIS and MOPITT.
- December 20 – The sovereignty of Macau is transferred from the Portuguese Republic to the People's Republic of China after 442 years of Portuguese settlement.
- December 22 – Korean Air Cargo Flight 8509, a Boeing 747-200F crashed shortly after take-off from London Stansted Airport due to pilot error. All 4 crew members were killed.
- December 24 – Indian Airlines Flight 814 was hijacked in Indian airspace between Kathmandu, Nepal and Delhi, India; landed at Amritsar, India; Lahore, Pakistan; Dubai; and Kandahar, Afghanistan. The ordeal lasted for 7 days.
- December 26 – Storm Lothar killed 137 people as it crossed France, southern Germany, and Switzerland.
- December 27 – Storm Martin caused damage throughout France, Spain, Switzerland and Italy, including an emergency due to flooding at the Blayais Nuclear Power Plant.
- December 30 – Former Beatle George Harrison was attacked at his home in Friar Park by 36-year-old Michael Abram.
- December 31
  - The U.S. turned over complete administration of the Panama Canal to the Panamanian Government, as stipulated in the Torrijos–Carter Treaties of 1977.
  - Boris Yeltsin resigned as President of Russia, leaving Prime Minister Vladimir Putin as the acting President.

- ○ Hijacking of Indian Airlines Flight 814 ended with the release of all but one of the crew and passengers at Kandahar Airport, Afghanistan.

Births

January–March

Madison Beer

- January 1 – Diamond White, American singer
- January 9 – Li Zhuhao, Chinese swimmer
- January 18
    - ○ Karan Brar, American actor
    - ○ Mateus Ward, American actor
- February 10 – Tiffany Espensen, Chinese actress
- February 25 – Gianluigi Donnarumma, Italian fooballer
- March 5 – Madison Beer, American singer
- March 21 – Mélusine Mayance, French child actress
- March 31 – Sawyer Fredericks, American singer-songwriter, winner of *The Voice* season 8

April–June

Isaac Hempstead Wright

- April 1 – Jairus Aquino, Filipino actor
- April 6 – Kwesi Boakye, American actor
- April 9 – Isaac Hempstead Wright, English actor
- April 18 – Michael Andrew, American swimmer
- May 11 – Sabrina Carpenter, American actress
- May 28 – Cameron Boyce, American actor
- June 2 – Madison Leisle, American actress
- June 20 – Yui Mizuno, Japanese singer/dancer (Babymetal)
- June 27 – Chandler Riggs, American actor

July–September

- July 4 – Moa Kikuchi, Japanese singer/dancer (Babymetal)
- July 9 – Claire Corlett, Canadian teen actress and singer
- July 20 – Princess Alexandra of Hanover
- July 30 – Joey King, American actress
- August 4 – Kelly Gould, American actress
- August 19 - Ethan Cutkosky, American actor
- August 22 – Dakota Goyo, Canadian actor

- August 28 – Prince Nikolai of Denmark
- September 7 – Michelle Creber, Canadian teen actress and singer
- September 14 - Emma Kenney, American actress
- September 30 – Flávia Saraiva, Brazilian artistic gymnast

October–December

- October 14 – Daniel Roche, British actor
- October 15 – Bailee Madison, American actress
- November 10 – Kiernan Shipka, American actress
- November 14 – Ellis Hollins, British actor

Deaths

January

- January 6 – Michel Petrucciani, French jazz pianist and composer (b. 1962)
- January 11
  - Fabrizio De André, Italian singer and songwriter (b. 1940)
  - Brian Moore, Irish-born writer (b. 1921)
- January 14 – Jerzy Grotowski, Polish theatre director (b. 1933)
- January 21 –
  - Susan Strasberg, American actress (b. 1938)

- Gerda Ring, Norwegian stage actress and stage producer (b. 1891)
- January 22 – Graham Staines, Australian missionary (b. 1941)
- January 25 – Robert Shaw, American conductor (b. 1916)
- January 28 – Markey Robinson, Irish painter (b. 1918)
- January 31 – Norm Zauchin, American baseball player (b. 1929)

February

Hussein of Jordan

Glenn T. Seaborg

- February 1
  - Paul Mellon, American philanthropist (b. 1907)

- Barış Manço, Turkish singer and television personality (b. 1943)
- February 5 – Wassily Leontief, Russian economist, Nobel Prize laureate (b. 1906)
- February 6
  - Jimmy Roberts, American singer (b. 1924)
  - Don Dunstan, Australian politician (b. 1926)
- February 7 – King Hussein of Jordan (b. 1935)
- February 8 – Iris Murdoch, Irish author (b. 1919)
- February 9 – Bryan Mosley, English actor (b. 1931)
- February 12 – Heinz Schubert, German actor, drama teacher and photographer (b. 1925)
- February 14 – John Ehrlichman, American Watergate scandal figure (b. 1925)
- February 15
  - Henry Way Kendall, American physicist, Nobel Prize laureate (b. 1926)
  - Big L, American rapper (b. 1974)
- February 17 – Sunshine Parker, American actor (b. 1927)
- February 18
  - Andreas Feininger, French-born photographer (b. 1906).
  - Noam Pitlik, American actor and director (b. 1932)
- February 20
  - Sarah Kane, English playwright (b. 1971)
  - Gene Siskel, American film critic (b. 1946)
- February 21 – Gertrude B. Elion, American scientist, recipient of the Nobel Prize in Physiology or Medicine (b. 1918)
- February 22 – William Bronk, American poet (b. 1918)

- February 24
  - Andre Dubus, American short-story writer (b. 1936)
  - Virginia Foster Durr, American civil rights activist (b. 1903)
  - Frank Leslie Walcott, Barbadian labour leader (b. 1916)
- February 25 – Glenn Seaborg, American chemist, Nobel Prize laureate (b. 1912)
- February 26 – José Quintero, Panamanian director (b. 1924)
- February 28 – Bill Talbert, American tennis player (b. 1918)

March

Dusty Springfield

Stanley Kubrick

Joe DiMaggio

Yehudi Menuhin

- March 1 – Ann Corio, American dancer and actress (b. 1914)
- March 2 – Dusty Springfield, English singer (b. 1939)
- March 3 – Gerhard Herzberg, German-born chemist, Nobel Prize laureate (b. 1904)
- March 4
  - Harry Blackmun, American judge (b. 1908)
  - Del Close, American actor, writer, and teacher (b. 1934)
- March 5

- o Alfred Denning, Baron Denning, British lawyer and judge (b. 1899)
- o John Figueroa, Jamaican poet (b. 1920)
- o Richard Kiley, American actor (b. 1922)
- March 7
  - o Sidney Gottlieb, American Central Intelligence Agency official (b. 1918)
  - o Stanley Kubrick, American film director and producer (b. 1928)
- March 8 – Joe DiMaggio, American baseball player (b. 1914)
- March 12 – Yehudi Menuhin, American-born violinist (b. 1916)
- March 13 – Garson Kanin, American playwright and screenwriter (b. 1912)
- March 17 – Ernest Gold, Austrian-born composer (b. 1921)
- March 18 – Adolfo Bioy Casares, Argentine writer (b. 1914)
- March 21 – Ernie Wise, English comedian (b. 1925)
- March 26 – David Holliday, British actor (b. 1937)
- March 29 – Joe Williams, American singer (b. 1918)
- March 31 – Yuri Knorozov, Russian linguist and epigrapher (b. 1922)

April

- April 3 – Lionel Bart, English composer (b. 1930)
- April 4
  - o Faith Domergue, American actress (b. 1924)
  - o Bob Peck, British actor (b. 1945)
- April 10 – Jean Vander Pyl, American television actress (b. 1919)

- April 12 – Boxcar Willie, American country music singer (b. 1931)
- April 14
  - Ellen Corby, American actress (b. 1911)
  - Anthony Newley, English actor, singer and songwriter (b. 1931)
- April 20
  - Rick Rude, American professional wrestler (b. 1958)
  - Señor Wences, Spanish ventriloquist (b. 1896)
- April 21 – Charles "Buddy" Rogers, American silent film actor (b. 1904)
- April 25
  - Lord Killanin, Irish journalist and Olympic official (b. 1914)
  - Herman Miller, American screenwriter and producer (b. 1919)
- April 26
  - Adrian Borland, British musician and producer (The Sound) (b. 1957)
  - Jill Dando, British television journalist (b. 1961)
- April 27
  - Al Hirt, American trumpeter and bandleader (b. 1922)
  - Cyril Washbrook, English cricketer (b. 1914)
- April 28
  - Rory Calhoun, American television and film actor (b. 1922)
  - Arthur Leonard Schawlow, American physicist, Nobel Prize laureate (b. 1921)
  - Sir Alf Ramsey World Cup winning football manager (b. 1920)

May

- May 2 – Oliver Reed, English actor (b. 1938)
- May 3 – Steve Chiasson, Canadian ice hockey player (b. 1967)
- May 8
  - Dirk Bogarde, English actor (b. 1921)
  - Dana Plato, American actress (b. 1964)
  - Soeman Hs, Indonesian author and educator (b. 1904)
- May 10
  - Shel Silverstein, American author and poet (b. 1930)
  - Eric Willis, Australian politician, former Premier of New South Wales (b. 1922)
- May 12 – Saul Steinberg, Romanian-born cartoonist (b. 1914)
- May 13 – Gene Sarazen, American golfer (b. 1902)
- May 17 – Henry Jones, American actor (b. 1912)
- May 18 – Betty Robinson, American athlete (b. 1911)
- May 19
  - Alister Williamson, Australian actor (b. 1918)
  - Candy Candido, American voice actor (b. 1913)
- May 23
  - Owen Hart, Canadian professional wrestler (b. 1965)
  - John T. Hayward, American admiral (b. 1908)
- May 26
  - Paul Sacher, Swiss conductor (b. 1906)
  - Waldo Semon, American inventor (b. 1898)

June

DeForest Kelley

Siegfried Lowitz

- June 5 – Mel Tormé, American singer (b. 1925)
- June 6 – Anne Haddy, Australian actress (b. 1930)
- June 9 – Maurice Journeau, French composer (b. 1898)
- June 11 – DeForest Kelley, American actor (b. 1920)
- June 16 – Screaming Lord Sutch, English politician (b. 1940)
- June 23 – Buster Merryfield, British Actor (b. 1920)
- June 25 – Fred Feast, English actor (b. 1929)
- June 27
    - Isaac C. Kidd, Jr., American admiral (b. 1919)
    - Siegfried Lowitz, German television actor (b. 1914)
    - Jorgos Papadopoulos, military ruler of Greece (b. 1919)
- June 29 – Allan Carr, American producer (b. 1937)

July

Sylvia Sidney

John F. Kennedy, Jr.

Hassan II of Morocco

- July 1
  - Dennis Brown, "Prince of Reggae", Singer (b. 1957)
  - Edward Dmytryk, Canadian-American film director (b. 1908)
  - Guy Mitchell, American singer (b. 1927)
  - Sylvia Sidney, American actress (b. 1910)
- July 2 – Mario Puzo, American author (b. 1920)
- July 4 – Jack Watson, English actor (b. 1915)
- July 6
  - Carl Gunter, Jr., American politician (b. 1938)
  - Joaquín Rodrigo, Spanish composer (b. 1901)
- July 7 – Julie Campbell Tatham, American writer (b. 1908)
- July 8 – Charles Conrad, American astronaut (b. 1930)
- July 11 – Helen Forrest, American jazz singer (b. 1917)
- July 16 – John F. Kennedy, Jr., American actor and son of John F. Kennedy (b. 1960)
- July 19 – Jerold Wells, English actor (b. 1908)
- July 20 – Sandra Gould, American actress (b. 1916)
- July 23 – King Hassan II of Morocco (b. 1929)
- July 28 – Trygve Haavelmo, Norwegian economist, Nobel Prize laureate (b. 1911)
- July 29
  - Anita Carter, American singer (b. 1933)
  - Rajendra Kumar, Indian film actor, producer and director (b. 1929)

August

- August 1 – Nirad C. Chaudhuri, Bengali writer (b. 1897)
- August 3 – Leroy Vinnegar, American musician (b. 1928)

- August 4 – Victor Mature, American actor (b. 1913)
- August 10
    - Anthony Stanislas Radziwill, American television executive and filmmaker (b. 1959)
    - Giuseppe Delfino, Italian fencer and Olympic champion in épée competition (b. 1921)
- August 14 – Lane Kirkland, American union leader (b. 1922)
- August 17 - Reiner Klimke, German equestrian (b. 1936)
- August 23
    - Norman Wexler, American screenwriter (b. 1926)
    - James White, Irish writer (b. 1928)
- August 24 – Mary Jane Croft, American actress (b. 1916)
- August 25 – Rob Fisher, British keyboardist, songwriter, member of Naked Eyes and Climie Fisher (b. 1956)

September

Marion Zimmer Bradley

- September 5 – Allen Funt, American television personality (b. 1914)
- September 6 – Lagumot Harris, Nauruan politician and former President (b. 1938)
- September 7 – Jim Keith, American author (b. 1949)
- September 9 – Ruth Roman, American actress (b. 1922)

- September 10 – Alfredo Kraus, Spanish tenor (b. 1927)
- September 11 – Gonzalo Rodríguez, Uruguayan racing driver (b. 1972)
- September 12 – Allen Stack, American Olympic swimmer (b. 1928)
- September 14 – Charles Crichton, English film director (b. 1910)
- September 20 – Raisa Gorbachova, Soviet first lady (b. 1932)
- September 22 – George C. Scott, American actor (b. 1927)
- September 23 – Ivan Goff, Australian screenwriter (b. 1910)
- September 25 - Marion Zimmer Bradley, American writer (b. 1930)

October

Wilt Chamberlain

Julius Nyerere

- October 3 – Akio Morita, Japanese businessman, co-founder of Sony (b. 1921)
- October 4
  - Bernard Buffet, French painter (b. 1928)
  - Art Farmer, American jazz trumpeter (b. 1928)
- October 6
  - Amália Rodrigues, Portuguese Fado legend (b. 1920)
  - Gorilla Monsoon, American professional wrestler and announcer (b. 1937)
- October 7 – Helen Vinson, American actress (b. 1907)
- October 8 – John McLendon, American basketball coach (b. 1915)
- October 9
  - Akhtar Hameed Khan, Pakistani pioneer in microcredit and microfinance (b. 1914)
  - Milt Jackson, American musician (b. 1923)
- October 11 – Rafi Daham al-Tikriti, Director of the Iraqi Intelligence Service (b. 1937)

- October 12 – Wilt Chamberlain, American basketball player (b. 1936)
- October 14 – Julius Nyerere, President of Tanzania (b. 1922)
- October 19
  - Harry Bannink, Dutch composer and musician (b. 1929)
  - James C. Murray, American politician (b. 1917)
  - Nathalie Sarraute, Russian-born Francophone lawyer and writer (b. 1900)
- October 20 – Jack Lynch, Taoiseach of Ireland (b. 1917)
- October 21
  - Lars Bo, Danish artist and writer (b. 1924)
  - John Bromwich, Australian tennis player (b. 1918)
- October 24 – John Chafee, American politician (b. 1922)
- October 25 – Payne Stewart, American golfer (b. 1957)
- October 26
  - Rex Gildo, German singer (b. 1939)
  - Hoyt Axton, American actor and singer-songwriter (b. 1938)
  - Abraham Polonsky, American screenwriter and director (b. 1910)
- October 27
  - Frank De Vol, American arranger, composer, and actor (b. 1911)
  - Robert Mills, American physicist (b. 1927)
- October 31 – Greg Moore, Canadian race car driver (b. 1975)

November

- November 1
  - Theodore Hall, American physicist and spy (b. 1925)

- o Walter Payton, American football player (b. 1953)
- November 3 – Ian Bannen, Scottish actor (b. 1928)
- November 9 – Mabel King, American actress (b. 1932)
- November 11
  - o Mary Kay Bergman, American actress (b. 1961)
  - o Vivian Fuchs, English geologist (b. 1908)
  - o Jacobo Timerman, Argentine journalist and author (b. 1923)
- November 12 – Mohammad Mohammadullah, 3rd President of Bangladesh (b. 1921)
- November 15 – Gene Levitt, American television writer, producer, and director (b. 1920)
- November 16 – Daniel Nathans, American microbiologist, recipient of the Nobel Prize in Physiology or Medicine (b. 1928)
- November 18
  - o Paul Bowles, American novelist (b. 1910)
  - o Horst P. Horst, German-American photographer (b. 1906)
  - o Doug Sahm, American musician (b. 1941)
- November 21 – Quentin Crisp, English writer (b. 1908)
- November 27 – Jim Wiggins, English actor (b. 1922)
- November 29
  - o Gene Rayburn, American television personality (b. 1917)
  - o Iwamoto Kaoru, Japanese professional Go player (b. 1902)

December

Rex Allen

Desmond Llewelyn

João Figueiredo

- December 2
  - Joey Adams, American comedian (b. 1911)
  - Charlie Byrd, American Jazz musician and classical guitarist (b. 1925)
- December 3
  - Scatman John, American musician (b. 1942)
  - Madeline Kahn, American actress (b. 1942)
- December 4 – Rose Bird, American judge (b. 1936)
- December 8
  - Péter Kuczka, Hungarian author (b. 1923)
  - Pupella Maggio, Italian actress (b. 1910)
- December 10
  - Rick Danko, Canadian musician (b. 1943)
  - Franjo Tuđman, President of Croatia (b. 1922)
- December 12
  - Paul Cadmus, American artist (b. 1904)
  - Joseph Heller, American novelist (b. 1923)
- December 17
  - Rex Allen, American actor, singer, and songwriter (b. 1920)
  - Grover Washington, Jr., American saxophonist (b. 1943)
- December 18 – Robert Bresson, French filmmaker (b. 1901)
- December 19
  - Desmond Llewelyn, Welsh actor (b. 1914)
  - Robert Dougall, British newsreader (b. 1913)
- December 20
  - Irving Rapper, American film director (b. 1898)
  - Hank Snow, Canadian musician (b. 1914)
- December 23 – John P. Davies, American diplomat (b. 1908)
- December 24

- ○ Tito Guízar, Mexican singer and film actor (b. 1908)
- ○ João Figueiredo, former military President of Brazil (b. 1918)
- December 26 – Curtis Mayfield, American musician and composer (b. 1942)
- December 27 – Leonard Goldenson, American television executive (b. 1905)
- December 28 – Clayton Moore, American actor (b. 1914)
- December 30 - Sarah Knauss, American supercentenarian, and the oldest American ever (b. 1880)
- December 31 – Elliot Richardson, American Attorney General under Richard Nixon (b. 1920)

Date unknown

- Halil-Salim Jabara, Israeli Arab politician (b. 1913)
- Prabhakar Thokal, Indian cartoonist (b. 1927)
- Harold Tamblyn-Watts, British cartoonist (b. 1900)

Nobel Prizes

- Physics – Gerardus 't Hooft and Martinus J. G. Veltman
- Chemistry – Ahmed H. Zewail
- Physiology or Medicine – Günter Blobel
- Literature – Günter Grass
- Peace – Médecins Sans Frontières
- Bank of Sweden Prize in Economic Sciences in Memory of Alfred Nobel – Robert Mundell

In the News.

The **worlds population** exceeds Six Billion.

The world prepares for the **new millennium** parties and computers around the world run testing for the millennium bug which could cause wide scale disruption to business and infrastructure if not fixed.

The take up of the **Internet** and Mobile Phones around the world open up new opportunities for successful entrepreneurs.

Euro currency introducedon 1st January in 11 countries.

Great Britain Introduces the Minimum Hourly Wage Rate of all adults must be paid at least £3.60 an hour.

Lance Armstrong wins his first Tour de France.

The **Millennium Dome** opens in London.

Impeachment Proceedings are bought against President Bill Clinton.

Prince Edward marries commoner Sophie Rhys-Jones on June 19th at St. George's Chapel, Windsor.

Total Eclipse Of The Sun Is Seen In cities of Europe and Asia.

Bluetooth announced.

Popular Films - Star Wars Episode I: The Phantom Menace, The Sixth Sense, Toy Story 2, The Matrix, Tarzan, The Mummy, Notting Hill.

Popular Television – Simpsons, Beverly Hills 90210, One Foot in the Grave (UK),Frasier, The X-Files, Chicago Hope, ER, Friends.

1999 Calendar.

January 1999
Sun	Mon	Tue	Wed	Thu	Fri	Sat
					1	2
3	4	5	6	7	8	9
10	11	12	13	14	15	16
17	18	19	20	21	22	23
24	25	26	27	28	29	30
31						

February 1999
Sun	Mon	Tue	Wed	Thu	Fri	Sat
	1	2	3	4	5	6
7	8	9	10	11	12	13
14	15	16	17	18	19	20
21	22	23	24	25	26	27
28						

March 1999
Sun	Mon	Tue	Wed	Thu	Fri	Sat
	1	2	3	4	5	6
7	8	9	10	11	12	13
14	15	16	17	18	19	20
21	22	23	24	25	26	27
28	29	30	31			

April 1999
Sun	Mon	Tue	Wed	Thu	Fri	Sat
				1	2	3
4	5	6	7	8	9	10
11	12	13	14	15	16	17
18	19	20	21	22	23	24
25	26	27	28	29	30	

May 1999
Sun	Mon	Tue	Wed	Thu	Fri	Sat
						1
2	3	4	5	6	7	8
9	10	11	12	13	14	15
16	17	18	19	20	21	22
23	24	25	26	27	28	29
30	31					

June 1999
Sun	Mon	Tue	Wed	Thu	Fri	Sat
		1	2	3	4	5
6	7	8	9	10	11	12
13	14	15	16	17	18	19
20	21	22	23	24	25	26
27	28	29	30			

July 1999
Sun	Mon	Tue	Wed	Thu	Fri	Sat
				1	2	3
4	5	6	7	8	9	10
11	12	13	14	15	16	17
18	19	20	21	22	23	24
25	26	27	28	29	30	31

August 1999
Sun	Mon	Tue	Wed	Thu	Fri	Sat
1	2	3	4	5	6	7
8	9	10	11	12	13	14
15	16	17	18	19	20	21
22	23	24	25	26	27	28
29	30	31				

September 1999
Sun	Mon	Tue	Wed	Thu	Fri	Sat
			1	2	3	4
5	6	7	8	9	10	11
12	13	14	15	16	17	18
19	20	21	22	23	24	25
26	27	28	29	30		

October 1999
Sun	Mon	Tue	Wed	Thu	Fri	Sat
					1	2
3	4	5	6	7	8	9
10	11	12	13	14	15	16
17	18	19	20	21	22	23
24	25	26	27	28	29	30
31						

November 1999
Sun	Mon	Tue	Wed	Thu	Fri	Sat
	1	2	3	4	5	6
7	8	9	10	11	12	13
14	15	16	17	18	19	20
21	22	23	24	25	26	27
28	29	30				

December 1999
Sun	Mon	Tue	Wed	Thu	Fri	Sat
			1	2	3	4
5	6	7	8	9	10	11
12	13	14	15	16	17	18
19	20	21	22	23	24	25
26	27	28	29	30	31